Official Selections

Fine Art
Portfolio

Decades of being around accomplished talent producing absolutely phenomenal quality work has taught that we are capable of greatness. It is possible to meet our destiny and become it. Experiencing excellence done with such apparent ease and humble selfless gratification is the motivation for this photography. Most important was having the freedom.

Joseph Fleming

Being colorblind gives an advantage when composing black & white… less confusion.
This special collection selected from thousands of captures. All images were framed
in the camera and presented without edits, genuine as seen through the lens.
RAW conversion applied by proprietary panchromatic process.
Limited fine art prints available from original files.

info@ BEACHNOISE.com

0351

0531

0705

0780

0826

0920

0938

1784

2467

3147

3359

3720

3799

4070

4099

4193

4265

4533

4560

4879

5492

5541

5750

5844

6095

6176

8173

8471

8889

9024

9975

9980

9992

www.ingramcontent.com/pod-product-compliance
Lightning Source LLC
Chambersburg PA
CBHW050744180526
45159CB00003B/1340